STALKING

By Lord Loveday Ememe and available from Lulu and Amazon.

The constitution and policing

Heresy

Starfleet

The supernatural

Creation

Deterrence

www.lulu.com

ISBN: 978-1-4717-7421-8

Table of Contents

1. THE SUPERNATURAL POWERS AND SENSES OF THE UNCIVILIZED

The supernatural powers and senses of the uncivilized are so enormous that it is extremely unreasonable to include or categorize the uncivilized as human beings according to the legal and moral definition of a man. It is also extremely relevant with regard to the commandment in the Bible to love your neighbour as yourself. This is in reference to the civil constitution of man; you cannot love the uncivilized as yourself if you are of a civilized nature, because there is a big difference between the civilized and uncivilized natures. If you are of a civilized nature, you will not want to have an uncivilized being as your neighbour because of the existence and dangers of their supernatural powers and senses, especially when they have demonstrated a willingness to misuse their supernatural powers and senses.

It is a wrong understanding or interpretation of the law for the uncivilized to believe that the civilized should have an open relationship with them because of their supernatural powers and senses, it is because of the toxicity of their supernatural powers and senses that there are strict guidelines governing direct or indirect contact with the civilized. This is a misinterpretation of the law, which is evidenced in their creation of Angels and demons and the unlawful practice of Angels being able to appear unannounced to someone of a civilized nature. This is a serious crime and a serious violation of the civil rights of the civilized. Supernaturalism is limited to the uncivilized for the purposes of law enforcement.

Compared to the senses of the civilized man, the supernatural powers and senses of the uncivilized are enormous. They have the power to change their physical appearance as well as the physical appearance of others. They have the power to know your private thoughts. They have the power to see into the future. These powers are similar but more extensive than magical powers. It is impossible for them to try to pass themselves off as civilized with these powers, in the same way that it is impossible for the civilized to pretend to be uncivilized with supernatural powers and senses, the uncivilized cannot pretend to be civilized. Although they are required by law for the purposes of law and order to exercise restraint with the use of these supernatural powers and senses because of its possible harmful effect on the civilized, the uncivilized and to a civilized society.

When you have the uncivilized with supernatural powers and super human strengths impersonating the civilized and unlawfully advocating hostile living conditions as suitable for the civilized because the uncivilized impersonating the civilized can cope with those harsh conditions they are attacking or persecuting the real civilized because the real civilized cannot cope with those living conditions because they are not the constitutional living conditions outlined in the constitution, the Christian principles, civil rights. Organized crime contrary to the misconception of its reference to the mafia is actually the current system of government in the world today, the uncivilized passing themselves off as civilized and assuming the constitutional roles of the civilized as rulers with devastating consequences. They have deliberately misinterpreted and misrepresented the constitution in order to cater to their barbaric sadistic natures. This includes laying the foundation to continuously stalk the civilized illegally, immorally, supernaturally for the rest of our lives, for one misguided purpose after another. These practices according to the guidance of the constitution are criminal activities that are extremely unhealthy for the civilized.

The uncivilized have powers that make them able to control the actions or behaviours of people similar to that of a remote control used to control the actions of robots. They can trigger behaviours or actions that appear voluntary but are actually outside the control of the individual. They not only know what you think but they can put thoughts in your head supernaturally that might appear voluntary but are actually involuntary.

Given the magnitude of the misuse of supernatural powers and senses by the uncivilized collectively to persecute the civilized before and after I became aware of the differences in their uncivilized natures and my civilized nature, they have collectively come up with an ingenious plan to sabotage my interest in films, music, radio and television to initiate indirectly illegal contact with me for unconstitutional political reasons in order to water down their past and present abominations involving the unlawful use of their supernatural powers and senses. This creates false impressions and also undermines the constitutional authority of the civilized like me. There is nothing to gain from these illegal supernatural alterations to my interests for the civilized like me other than to cater to the sadistic barbaric nature of the uncivilized.

The supernatural powers and senses of the uncivilized mean that any situation they are in, they are not in the situation in good faith, unlike the civilized, because of the lack of supernatural powers and senses any situation we are in, we are in that situation in good faith. This is the reasoning behind the lack of forgiveness for the uncivilized in the constitution, the reason why the civilized are the only ones that can be forgiven in the constitution, is a lesson for the uncivilized to understand that the existence of the differences means that it is impossible to blame the civilized for situations that are easily avoidable by the uncivilized. So when the uncivilized think that they can get away with the direct or indirect misuse of their supernatural powers to harm the civilized, whether they pretend to be civilized or not, it will be interpreted by the constitution regardless of their misguided purposes as serious crimes, which they will be severely punished for.

The constitution, which is the Christian principles, civil rights, considers the supernatural powers and senses of the uncivilized as massive compared to the civilized nature and as a consequence considers the lack of supernatural powers and senses of the civilized nature as an enormous sacrifice. The constitution does not allow the uncivilized to undermine the enormous sacrifice of the civilized nature by the unlawful interference with the administrative or civil powers or the right of dominion over this universe of the civilized nature.

The uncivilized unlawfully altered the constitutional living conditions for the civilized nature, in order to unlawfully supernaturally stalk the civilized under the guise of help and protection for one misguided purpose after another for problems that the uncivilized are collectively responsible for.

In line with the guidance of the constitution, before I became aware of the differences that were kept from me between the civilized nature and the uncivilized, before I became a teenager I was confirmed in an African (Nigerian) traditional ceremony as a commissioner of the metropolitan police force (Eze Okonko). This confirmation by the constitution and an African traditional ceremony as a commissioner of the metropolitan police force has not been replicated illegally in my country of birth, the United Kingdom. I can only conclude that it is for discriminatory, persecutory reasons by the white race in England, towards the civilized, especially if you of African origin like me. It is strange that the white race will be the first to try to express concern for your welfare illegally, supernaturally, unhealthily for the civilized. They express false concern for your welfare in an unhealthy way, supernaturally, which is unconstitutional. The white race are also the first to try to sabotage your interests supernaturally to initiate illegal communications or relationships with the civilized to create false impressions for political reasons to further their demonism. It is amazing that they are trying to compromise the civilized even more by trying to elect police commissioners illegally (amongst the uncivilized), contrary to the guidance of the constitution. Interfering illegally with the constitutional rights of the civilized. It is similar to prisoners electing a prison warden from amongst themselves. A police commissioner is the civilized nature or constitution, it is not the uncivilized nature and the uncivilized are not allowed to impersonate a police commissioner because it defeats the purpose of the constitution, the Christian principles.

The history of the white race with those different from them, if they are unfortunate and the white race gets emotionally entangled with them, it means oppression, persecution, loss of rights and privileges because they like to enslave different cultures to their demonism.

It makes no difference what your skin colour is, if you are of an uncivilized nature you cannot be a police commissioner. The differences in the uncivilized nature and the civilized nature mean that the duties of a police commissioner are not as involved as the uncivilized make out. Bearing in mind that the constitution defines work as the use of supernatural powers and senses, which the civilized do not have.

The deliberate undermining of the constitutional rights of the civilized by the uncivilized is as a result of the perverted emotional entanglements developed from the constant unlawful supernatural stalking of the civilized by the uncivilized.

History's serious warnings about the extremely dangerous nature of the white race and their demonic practice of stalking those different from even in their own countries have been seriously understated.

The misuse of supernatural powers and senses by the uncivilized, stalking, to undermine my constitutional authority or civil rights, thereby creating lawlessness means that I have been made a political prisoner. When I go out I am constantly being exposed to unlawful supernaturalism because of the lack of policing.

The misuse of supernatural powers and senses by the uncivilized, stalking, to unlawfully incorporate death, illnesses and ageing into the life span of the civilized contrary to the guidance of the constitution, means that the civilized are meant to live our lives in a very horrific way that was never envisaged by the constitution, to expect death or illness at any time. This caters to the sadistic nature of the uncivilized, the civilized are meant to expect to be assassinated or abused at any time unlawfully by the uncivilized.

The uncivilized need to understand that according to the guidance of the constitution, which is the Christian principles, civil rights they must comply completely with the instructions of the constitution, there is no middle ground. They are either with God the law or they are not. Those that live in glass houses do not throw stones.

Stalking supernaturally by the uncivilized the civilized includes the uncivilized misusing their supernatural powers and senses to put themselves between the civilized and what the civilized want in different ways with regard to access to goods and services.

The salary rights privileges immunity from prosecution (similar in principle to diplomatic immunity) for a real commissioner of police without their association to disability is relevant to the establishment and maintenance of universal peace and security and the confirmation of the identities of the civilized. It helps prevent the civilized from being forced into role plays aimed at catering to the sadism of the uncivilized. Without these constitutional security measures the civilized will constantly be stalked supernaturally by the uncivilized which is unhealthy for the civilized and similar to being constantly raped and paedophilia, contrary to the instructions of the constitution.

The uncivilized have the powers to make the civilized dream about anything similar to hypnosis, the same way our interests like films, music have been altered supernaturally to enable direct or indirect illegal communications with the civilized. In light of these forms of stalking it is unreasonable to suggest that the civilized should not sleep in case of supernatural interference with our dreams or to suggest that the civilized are doing something wrong because of circumstances outside our control, if we decide to sleep. This also applies to our interests, like films and music. The solution is to have a police force operating within the guidelines of the constitution that should be able to police these activities and help prevent or deter the misuse of supernatural powers and senses.

Contrary to the misconception developed by the current criminal activities by the uncivilized, government ministers or prophets are of the civilized nature or constitution (without supernatural powers and senses). This also applies to the misconception of the idea of an angel or God, that an angel can observe certain things going on that are criminal activities and do not interfere like a revered statute, it is not a reference to the uncivilized with supernatural powers and senses but a reference to the civilized without supernatural powers and senses. The uncivilized and their illegal persistence to draw the civilized into their unlawful unhealthy role plays, behave like comedians or rapists that cannot accept that they are not funny or friendly but extremely toxic, and then want to force themselves on the civilized.

According to the guidance of the constitution regarding the reasoning behind the purpose of Angels, in my legal (constitutional) capacity as a commissioner (judge), their actions do not fit the psychological profile of Angels or God. The creator in the Garden of Eden provided the psychological profile of a mentally fit supernatural or uncivilized, with regard to the relationship between the civilized and the uncivilized. According to the psychological profile of a mentally fit supernatural provided by the creator, a supernatural that directly or indirectly through action or inaction undermines the constitutional authority of the civilized has a severe mental disorder and is a danger to themselves and those around them.

A character in a film, a low down dirty shame, played by Jada Pinkett-Smith was a fan of an American TV soap opera; the character disagreed with a story line and was not happy with the behaviour of a fictional character in the TV soap opera. The character played by Jada Pinkett-Smith saw the actor in the TV soap opera and attacked him because she was not happy with the behaviour of the fictional character the actor plays in the TV soap opera. This can be categorized as a mild type of stalking.

Then imagine the lives of the civilized that are being stalked constantly supernaturally by psychopaths with supernatural powers and senses, that monitor everything we do, bearing in mind that everyone has an opinion about how to go about doing different things, the civilized cannot commit crimes because of the lack of supernatural powers and senses so the psychopaths torture the civilized because of a difference of opinion about issues that are private and personal to the civilized. The private thoughts of the civilized are being monitored by these psychopaths with supernatural powers and senses.

According to the guidance of the constitution, no supernatural should be in receipt of a salary higher than the civilized. This is in acknowledgement of the instructions of the constitution confirming the civilized as rulers or Administrators.

Taxation is not a necessity but a symbolic tool to maintain law and order in a civilized society, although it is being misused by the uncivilized for illegal stalking purposes. Taxation is a symbolic acknowledgement of the relationship between the uncivilized and the civilized, formulated in the Garden of Eden. Under no circumstances are the civilized to be taxed for anything, because it will undermines the purpose of the constitution and the distinction between the civilized and uncivilized.

2. THE HARMFUL PSYCHOLOGICAL EFFECTS OF SUPERNATURALISM ON THE CIVILIZED

The uncivilized have unlawfully created warlike living conditions around the world that caters to their barbaric sadistic natures, at the expense of international peace and security and the mental and physical wellbeing of the civilized. These warlike living conditions are reflected in the unnecessary illegal adversarial system of government politics, the unnecessary unlawful adversarial legal systems that only serves to promote lawlessness and the persecution of the civilized. Protestations and complaints go in one ear and out the next. The only complaints they are interested in are those that are compatible with the warlike living conditions. This means that the civilized are unlawfully excluded from society, life having been deliberately made impossible, making the civilized dependent on the charity or goodwill of psychopaths. This is psychologically extremely harmful for the civilized.

When you have an illegitimate government that encourages the systematic execution of all its citizens with the misuse of supernatural powers and senses, by illegally incorporating death, ageing into the life span of its citizens illegally, it is psychologically harmful. There is a difference between a situation where there is no choice as the civilized were misled to believe and when others are illegally misusing their supernatural powers and senses to make life and death decisions for you. You are expected to live your life expecting to be murdered by the uncivilized at any time. You are also expected to live your live expecting to be made ill by the uncivilized at any time.

The uncivilized have supernaturally altered images in films and voices in music and made them supernatural, this means that the voices and images are aware of your private thoughts, are aware of you watching or listening which is illegal and unhealthy. This is a psychologically harmful type of stalking for the civilized. The computer graphics in video games look real and my experiences will suggest that the graphics could be illegally made to be living beings, which will be psychologically damaging for the civilized but taken differently by the uncivilized.

The constitution defines work as the use of supernatural powers and senses, which the civilized are naturally excluded from, and only instructs that the civilized are rulers or commissioners of police, nothing more and nothing less. When the uncivilized, psychopaths, start experimenting with their creation of a different work concept, they should limit the experiment amongst the uncivilized and should not try to abuse the civilized by forcing it on us directly or indirectly. Their new work concept given what is possible will suggest that it is a type of social activity for the uncivilized, which if forced on the civilized is similar to rape or paedophilia. When these psychopaths, the uncivilized try to misuse their supernatural powers and senses to make the livelihood of the civilized dependent on their work concept, it is a serious crime, and a horrific type of supernatural stalking.

The uncivilized should understand before developing or experimenting on new abusive ideas that in my official capacity as a commissioner of police (judge) their past deeds to date make them according to the guidance of the constitution fugitives from justice, until I decide otherwise.

The civilized are not mentally or severely mentally impaired regardless of the illegal efforts of the uncivilized, psychopaths, to create the false impression in order to undermine the constitutional authority of the civilized. The constitution confirms the psychological harmful effects of supernaturalism on the civilized with the creation of Eve for Adam, when Adam was protected from supernaturalism by being made to sleep when Eve was created in order to prevent the psychological harmful effects of supernaturalism on the civilized. The separation of powers civil and supernatural powers is essential to protect the mental and physical wellbeing of the civilized and establishes and maintains universal peace and security.

The uncivilized should understand that the civilized are not impressed with supernaturalism, we are more likely going to order the arrest of the uncivilized for breaching the peace with supernaturalism. According to the guidance of the constitution, the family is a curse, and the civilized are not allowed to be burdened with it. The family is a weapon that can be used by the uncivilized to try to compromise the constitutional authority of the civilized in order to maintain lawlessness. The uncivilized have been using the family concept to sensationalize the idea of death, life after death and the anticipation of seeing family members again. They like the idea of being worth dying for, which serves no purpose but caters to their sadistic natures and egos.

I have recently after over thirty years of watching films, realized that the images of some of the actors of different skin colours resemble family members. This will suggest that they are using the concept of the family to violate my civil rights. The images were suddenly turned to not only living things but supernatural, which is unlawful and unhealthy. They think that the violation of my civil rights is okay if done by family members contrary to the instructions of the constitution.

My experiences confirm that the uncivilized are self-absorbed psychopaths that are willing to hide behind the family concept to interfere with my constitutional authority in order to undermine my civil rights. According to the guidance of the constitution nothing including the family concept that applies only to the uncivilized can justify the misuse of supernatural powers and senses to harm mentally or physically the civilized, obstruct or delay the complete implementation of the constitutional authority of the civilized. The uncivilized misuse their supernatural powers and senses to damage my property, and try to hide behind wear and tear. I am aware that properties when built last for centuries. Nobody will build or buy a house if you need to keep on rebuilding or do extensive repairs, so my situation is as a consequence of being stalked constantly by the uncivilized. The only time you will need to do extensive repairs are when your property has been exposed to seriously harsh weather or flooding. The flooding has to be massive, and it is the contents in your property rather than your property that will be damaged. The weather problem is as a result of the misuse of their supernatural powers and senses.

It is possible that the uncivilized, psychopaths could deliberately create illegally horrific living conditions as my reality and be living in a different place like a planet, parallel universe or dimension. I do not have a problem with them living somewhere else, I welcome it. What I will have a problem with is the deliberate unlawful misuse of supernatural powers and senses to create horrific impossible living conditions for the civilized and after the damage go somewhere else to live. Contrary to the misconception, the constitutional sacred authority of the civilized extends to all parts of the universe. The drama series charmed which is meant to be fiction but reveals their supernaturalism and the possibilities of different dimensions or parallel universe, confirms its possibility.

The serious differences between the civilized and uncivilized mean that it is impossible for the civilized to be hostile towards the uncivilized or touch the uncivilized in a hostile manner unless the uncivilized misuse their supernatural powers and senses to create false impressions. So attacks on the civilized by the uncivilized whether the uncivilized think they are joking or playing games will be interpreted by the constitution as serious unprovoked attacks which are serious crimes. Because supernaturalism regardless of how it is presented is psychologically harmful to the civilized.

The uncivilized will concede the obvious fact that they find the uncivilized themselves a serious problem and need some order to get a bit of peace. So they should not delude themselves into believing that they are doing the civilized a favour or helping the civilized by implementing completely the instructions of the constitution. The uncivilized should stop getting emotional or political with the implementation of the instructions of the constitution.

Their emotional or political dramatics are extremely unhealthy for the civilized, and undermines international peace and security.

The constitution, which is the Christian principles, civil rights, its sole purpose, is to protect the constitutional authority of the civilized from the uncivilized. So when the uncivilized pretend to be of the civilized nature and take away the constitutional authority of the civilized, they are undermining a sacred constitution. They are challenging the essence of Christianity or the law.

The media that are actively supporting illegitimate governments of the uncivilized pretending to be civilized at the expense of law and order are party to challenging the essence of the law or Christianity. They cannot serve two masters, they are either with the law God or they are not. The uncivilized collectively try to intimidate and discredit the civilized in order to take away illegally the constitutional authority of the civilized. The point of the law, the civilized, is to regulate the actions of the uncivilized. The uncivilized are not allowed to impersonate the civilized to deny the civilized our constitutional authority to rule, because it defeats the purpose of the law.

I am forty years old and only found out that I was surrounded by people different from me with supernatural powers and senses in 1998/99. Although I was always aware of the existence and dangers of supernatural powers and senses from my education at an Anglican seminary school, those around me hid the differences and also instigated doubts in me about the authenticity of my seminary education.

I had an unauthorized visit to my home in 2011 from a doctor at a doctor's surgery I had informed that I no longer wanted to be registered with. This was a deliberate conspiracy by the uncivilized collectively given the current state of affairs to provoke a reaction from me. I refused the doctor entry to my home, although I informed the police of the unauthorized visit, the doctor managed to convince the police to have me illegally sectioned under a non-existent Mental Health Act. This was clearly the uncivilized ganging up on me to say indirectly that I am at their mercy, like a slave and a slave master. I was illegally taken to a mental health unit where I was surrounded by the uncivilized, both the patients, doctors, nurses were all super naturals. In 2000/2001 my concerns and complaints about being surrounded by the uncivilized with supernatural powers and senses were dismissed as hallucinations and as a consequence I was unlawfully diagnosed as suffering from a severe mental disorder which is permanent. And the uncivilized want to unlawfully initiate conversations, contacts based on this destructive lie about their identities. These unnecessary problems are evidence of their demonic practices of show without substance. When you are being stalked supernaturally by these uncivilized psychopaths they start getting emotionally entangled with you and try to force uninvited, unwanted, unhealthy contact. Unfortunately they use themselves as a measure to determine what they think the civilized will want, when there is a massive difference, they pretend to be civilized and after a while they really believe they are at the expense of the physical and mentally wellbeing of the real civilized like me. When they supernaturally damage your property and try to pretend it is wear and tear or accidental and you make efforts to repair it yourself, they supernaturally interfere with your efforts because they prefer the show no substance option of one of them doing the repairs at the expense of your mental and physical wellbeing. My physical, mental and financial wellbeing are always compromised for their demonism of show without substance.

According to the guidance of the constitution, without the proper implementation of the constitutional authority, civil or administrative powers of the civilized, the civilized are unlawfully incomplete and have been rendered deliberately disabled by the uncivilized psychopaths. This also means that without our civil powers, it is unlawful for the uncivilized to initiate direct or indirect contact with the civilized.

When the uncivilized supernaturally stalk the civilized unlawfully and we have a routine that suits us but the uncivilized have a different opinion, they supernaturally try to interfere with your private business to force their opinion on you, it makes no difference to them that your right to privacy is being violated, although unlawful, it is also unhealthy for the civilized, psychologically damaging. They end up creating a problem because of a difference of opinion.

Adam in the Garden of Eden was ruler of the world but he never had the chance to rule because of supernaturalism, he never made a single decision for himself, he was never allowed unlawfully to exercise his civil right to self-determination. The world has not recovered from that blunder.

The uncivilized misuse their supernatural powers and senses and put the civilized through psychologically damaging processes to create unwanted problems in our lives, if it is going to be corrected you will be taken through another psychologically damaging process like an inanimate object or toy for their sadistic pleasure or amusement.

The problem with the uncivilized, psychopaths and the misuse of their supernatural powers and senses is that they behave like heroin addicts that have lost the ability to reason and will try to justify criminal behaviour or activity in order to get a fix of heroin, the misuse of their supernatural powers and senses.

The uncivilized, psychopaths should understand the problems they face when they try to justify unprovoked attacks on the civilized, compared to the superhuman strengths(supernatural powers and senses) of the uncivilized the civilized are like statues and that is overstating the nature of the civilized given the supernatural powers and senses of the uncivilized. They become increasingly desperate to try to justify unprovoked attacks on the civilized, and try to hide behind jokes and games when no relationship exists. This means that the only way they have established a delusional relationship is supernaturally, which is unlawful and unhealthy for the civilized. The civilized are being stalked supernaturally by the illegal alterations to our interests like films, music and novels. The civilized are also being stalked supernaturally by the unlawful obstruction of our constitutional right to rule. When they illegally start anything supernaturally which will inevitably backfire, they try to blame the victims of their criminal activities, the civilized. The differences mean that although the uncivilized are aware that their actions are unlawful, they cannot fully comprehend the harmful psychological effects of supernaturalism on the civilized.

3. THE GENETIC FLAW OF THE UNCIVILIZED, POWER TRIPPING

The persecution, discriminatory practices of the uncivilized with regard to the civilized is done collectively by the uncivilized regardless of skin colour, age or their definition of biological family ties. They collectively enjoy their illegally obtained status of being superior to the civilized contrary to the guidance of the constitution.

The supernatural instincts of the uncivilized that led to the wrong interpretation of the constitution mean that direct or indirect contact with civilized will lead to the civilized being taken on a deadly rollercoaster ride. The uninvited, unwanted customization of services like radio broadcasts, television broadcasts, films and music for a civilized person watching or listening which relies on altering these services to make them supernatural is unlawful, unhealthy for the civilized and only serves the sadistic, psychopathic needs of the uncivilized.

The civil constitution or nature is more authentic but similar in principle to when someone is said to be born of noble blood or it is someone's birth right to govern. There are different ways to describe a civil constitution or nature; it can be referred to as police commissioner or ruler.

The salary of a commissioner of the metropolitan police force has been worked out as £260,000.00 per annum. This it appears only applies if a psychopathic supernatural impersonates the civilized. They have not quite worked it out yet that the constitution interprets the civilized constitution as a massive sacrifice for universal peace and security.

Both Adam and the creator were heavy weights with unique qualities, which the uncivilized have conspired to undermine. The revelation with the continuous problems in the universe is how extremely vital Adam's qualities were to the stability of the universe.

If you are of a civil constitution you cannot travel if you are not financially secure in case of emergencies, unless the uncivilized psychopaths want you to live your live through their eyes, which defeats the purpose of the sacred creation of the law, the civilized. The uncivilized cannot be civilized the same way the civilized cannot be supernatural, the civilized collectively cannot vote to have a civilized person assume the responsibilities of a supernatural, it is silly, the same way the uncivilized collectively cannot vote to have a supernatural assume the responsibilities of the civilized, it is silly in a self-destructive way. It is similar to women voting for one of their own to assume the bodily functions of a man or men voting for one of their own to assume the bodily functions of a woman. It just does not make senses and is extremely chaotic and undermines law and order.

For evil to triumph it is only sufficient for good men to do nothing. So given the state of the world and the persecuted state of the civilized are there no good super naturals?

The civilized do not suffer fools, if that impression was created it is as a collective conspiracy of the uncivilized psychopaths by the corruption of our education, which I moved on from once I became aware of the differences and the extreme wickedness of the uncivilized. It appears that it is the uncivilized psychopaths that were affected by the corruption because they are still trapped by it. They have not yet adjusted their method of communication or contact with the civilized given the legal fact that the civilized are the constitutional rulers or commissioners of police of this planet and universe.

The choices are simple; it is either a supernatural administration by the uncivilized psychopaths where there is lawlessness and no rights or a civil administration by the civilized with the correct identification, interpretation and application of the constitution with the proper establishment of a peace keeping force, which preserves individual rights and personal freedoms. It simply means a choice between war and peace. Supernaturalism represents war and lawlessness. Civilization represents peace and law and order.

According to the guidance of the constitution, the uncivilized do not speak for or represent the interest of the civilized, the current state of affairs in the world demands the unconditional surrender of the uncivilized masquerading as civilized and unlawfully denying the civilized our constitutional authority to govern, no terms. Any supernatural coming into my home supernaturally is doing that illegally, politically, in order to maintain the illegal status quo, this includes politicians.

Supernaturalism is an extremely aggressively type of stalking, and it is an understatement, regardless of how it is presented and its misguided purpose. Supernaturalism or stalking is about the domination and oppression of the weak or vulnerable. The uncivilized are intoxicated by power and create situations illegally to interfere in people's lives. It is unhealthy, and only serves to cater to the power tripping natures of the uncivilized psychopaths. Supernaturalism or stalking represents the uncivilized wanting to make decisions for the civilized and will go as far as creating extremely hostile conditions for the civilized to create false impressions which will suggest that the civilized are incapable of taking care of ourselves. This is a useful ploy with regard to the constitutional authority of the civilized to govern. It is confirmed by the constitution that illegal contacts with the civilized by the uncivilized outside the guidelines of the constitution mean that they are suffering from a severe mental disorder. This has been established by the psychological profile of a mentally fit supernatural in relation to their relationship with the civilized.

As a consequence of the moral or legal superiority of the civilized, the competitive nature of the uncivilized has made them collectively conspire to try to undermine the constitutional authority of the civilized. They have gone as far as to try to compare themselves to the civilized which is completely impossible with devastating consequences for the wellbeing of the civilized. With this in mind it is understandable why the constitution does not allow them to interfere or plan the lives of the civilized outside the guidelines of the constitution. They are only required to ensure that the constitutional living conditions of the civilized are in place and the identities of the civilized are confirmed officially as commissioners of the metropolitan police force to enable the civilized to live our lives independently and exercise our right to self-determination.

The uncivilized and the civilized do not have to like each other, it is not necessary, for the instructions of the constitution to be implemented completely, it is not a political issue, it is a legal issue. In any case politics is unconstitutional, and because of its link to public opinion, it represents the nature of the uncivilized. Politics is supernatural an extremely hazardous type of stalking.

Since becoming aware of the differences over ten years ago, between the uncivilized and the civilized like me, I have not had a supernatural friend or personal relationship with a supernatural and do not want to. Every contact or communication with a supernatural is exploited for political demonic purposes aimed at maintaining the unconstitutional status quo.

As it has become apparent that the uncivilized psychopaths have lost the legal or moral argument to govern, they try to force personal relationships with the civilized supernaturally, in order to create false impressions to maintain the unconstitutional status quo.

There are certain activities that the uncivilized take part in that given their supernatural powers and senses will make them severely mad, so they try to personalize the activities as if for the benefit or purpose of helping the civilized supernaturally, which then becomes a severe type of stalking and a serious health hazard for the civilized.

Familiarity associated with the supernatural powers and senses of the uncivilized breeds unprovoked contempt for the civilized, which is an aggressive type of stalking. This is because they are threatened by the constitutional authority of the civilized which exposes the uncivilized masquerading as civilized as frauds.

The harmful psychological effects of supernaturalism, stalking, on the civilized, are certification of the authenticity of the constitution's instruction that the civilized are by nature commissioners of the metropolitan police force.

I had made a reasonable effort to disassociate myself from the uncivilized once I became aware of the differences and their extreme wickedness involving the direct and indirect misuse of their supernatural powers and senses. Unfortunately they have altered my interests to force unwanted or uninvited interaction with images in films and voices in music, which is worse than rape and paedophilia. Not only have they illegally and immorally altered my interests they are trying to set rules associated with the alterations, so you either watch films or listen to music in conditions similar to wearing a biohazard suit or you give up your interests. This is an extreme type of stalking. This illegal supernatural stalking has led to these uncivilized psychopaths damaging my property supernaturally. The things they choose to supernaturally damage are meant to cause serious discomfort.

As a consequence of the civilized having no supernatural powers and senses, which means that we cannot hear or see the uncivilized and as a consequence considered snobs by the uncivilized, in order to gain our attention we are constantly being stalked supernaturally and we are violated supernaturally by the uncivilized and our properties are criminally damaged by the uncivilized supernaturally.

The monarchy centuries ago, in line with the constitution, the Christian principles, surrendered the administrative or civil powers of the civilized, not to the uncivilized, whether they are pretending to be civilized or not, but to the civilized to then commission the monarchy to police the uncivilized.

I have to concede that the monarchy in the United Kingdom against all the odds managed to maintain the link between the Christian principles or the civil constitution of man and the state or civilization. The surrendering of the civil or administrative powers of the civilized was never for political reasons as that is unconstitutional but for law and order. This simply means that the civilized, the living representations of the law, as commissioners of the metropolitan police force, the monarchy has more operational powers and not less, in order to adequately police the uncivilized.

Interfering with or obstructing the constitutional authority of the civilized including the rights, privileges, salaries, immunity from prosecution of the civilized as commissioners of the metropolitan police force is worse than taking food out of the mouth of a hungry baby or putting a baby in a very dangerous environment.

The uncivilized keep on procrastinating with the required implementation of the instructions of the constitution for power tripping purposes, as if they have a choice, contrary to the guidance of the constitution. In order to maintain the current unlawful practices they continue to deal only with the symptoms of a problem rather than the cause of the problem.

The civil list is money meant for the monarchy or a section of the monarchy as head of state or civilized society, which confirms the pivotal role of the civilized nature or the Christian principles. The Christian principles or the civilized constitution is the foundation of government; a civilized society is governed by the Christian principles or the civilized constitution. I believe that the position of the civilized as commissioners of the metropolitan police force fulfils the requirement of the constitution for reasons already stated.

According to the guidance of the constitution, the practice of politics is unconstitutional, a criminal activity, politics including political parties should be scrapped, abolished. The practice of politics creates a false impression that there is no constitution which breeds lawlessness and caters to the sadism of uncivilized psychopaths.

The uncivilized psychopaths should understand that there is no defence against the law which is a sacred creation.

When a supernatural is trying to communicate to a civilized person, directly or indirectly, to give them bad news or bad news about the future, the constitution interprets such actions by the supernatural as a very serious crime, an attack on the civilized person.

Misery or supernaturalism loves company; it undermines or compromises personal freedoms, individual rights, independence and the constitutional authority of the civilized.

There are two categories of supernatural unlawful intrusions for misguided purposes given the guidance of the constitution. The first group are those that have the characteristics of slave masters and want to enslave the civilized to stalking by exploiting deliberate vulnerabilities created by the misuse of supernatural powers and senses. They want to make the civilized dependent on illegal criminal activities. The second group are those with the characteristics of slaves, their misguided approach to helping the civilized illegally will inevitable have the unlawful effect of planning the lives of the civilized like the lives of slaves. It is as silly as trying to make a slave of their idea of a God. It is a serious abomination.

The uncivilized need to understand that the restrictions imposed on them for law and order reasons are because of their supernatural powers and senses, which mean that those restrictions do not apply to the civilized, the differences are massive, so the uncivilized should not compare their lives to the lives of the civilized.

The uncivilized psychopaths like to get involved in the private affairs of others uninvited, they do this supernaturally, stalking, when you make private plans they want to interfere with the timing or alter it completely for no other reason but for power tripping purposes.

The Christian principles, the constitution, have a universal appeal in providing universal peace and security, unlike supernaturalism that excludes completely the vulnerable and establishes and maintains lawlessness.

When I look at the cost of private jets, yachts, hotel suites, holidays that are safe for the civilized, according to what someone I knew in past once said, it appears that we have just escorted some people to this world. The civilized can never afford the life style the constitution instructs we are by law entitled to because the uncivilized have made sure that to achieve monetary success you must be supernatural or a slave to a supernatural. It is strange that according to the law, the uncivilized do not fall within the legal definition of a man; this means that the uncivilized do not have the legal status to own properties including money.

Accidents, threats and fear of accidents are creations of the uncivilized, while masquerading as civilized, with the misuse of their supernatural powers and senses to oppress or dominate those that are different from them, including the civilized.

It is naturally impossible for the civilized and the uncivilized to play games and joke with each other. This accounts for the psychologically harmful effects on the civilized of the games and jokes of the uncivilized, which the constitution will interpret as serious attacks on the civilized.

According to the guidance of the constitution, the misuse of supernatural powers and senses to harm the civilized, mentally or physically, is never forgiven.

4. AUTHOR'S NOTES

This is my seventh non-fiction book about the law. It is about what I believe to be the correct identification, interpretation and application of the constitution of the United Kingdom and the world. It exposes the conspiracy of the uncivilized, those with supernatural powers and senses, that are enslaving the world to extreme types of barbarism that caters to their sadistic natures. They unlawfully pretend to be civilized, those without supernatural powers and senses in order to deny the civilized our constitutional right to govern in order to create lawlessness that caters to their psychopathic sadistic natures. This extreme level of lawlessness that persecutes the vulnerable including the civilized would not have been possible without the collective deception of the uncivilized regardless of appearances.

5. AUTHOR'S BIOGRAPHY

.

My name is Lord Loveday Ememe. I was born in the United Kingdom. I am a graduate of an Anglican seminary school (the real police academy); I also graduated from the University of East London with an honours degree in law. I am of a civilized nature and as a consequence as confirmed by the constitution of the United Kingdom, a commissioner of the metropolitan police force. I was also confirmed in Nigeria by a traditional ceremony as a commissioner of the metropolitan police force because my biological parents are from Nigeria. For political, discriminatory persecutory reasons the white race in the United Kingdom have refused to accept the instructions of the constitution regarding my official confirmation as a commissioner of the metropolitan police force.

Bibliography

The Bible